MUSTARD

By Eva O'Connor

FOR AMATEUR PRODUCTION ENQUIRIES

UNITED KINGDOM AND WORLD
EXCLUDING NORTH AMERICA
licensing@concordtheatricals.co.uk
020-7054-7200

Each title is subject to availability from Concord Theatricals, depending upon country of performance.

MUSIC USE NOTE

IMPORTANT BILLING AND CREDIT REQUIREMENTS

USE OF COPYRIGHT MUSIC

FIRST PERFORMANCE

MUSTARD premiered at Bruford, Summerhall at the Edinburgh Fringe in August 2019. The play is produced by Fishamble: The New Play Company, in association with Sunday's Child.

WINNER OF A SCOTSMAN FRINGE FIRST AWARD 2019
WINNER OF THE SUMMERHALL LUSTRUM AWARD 2019.
NOMINATED FOR SCOTTISH MENTAL HEALTH AWARD 2019.

Written and performed by	**Eva O'Connor**
Directed by	**Hildegard Ryan**
Set and costume design by	**Hildegard Ryan**
Lighting design by	**Marianne Nightingale**
Cover photo by	**Hildegard Ryan**

Fishamble Team

Artistic Director	**Jim Culleton**
Dramaturg	**Gavin Kostick**
Production Coordinator	**Ronan Carey**
Marketing	**Chandrika Narayanan-Mohan**
PR	**O'Doherty Communications**
Producer	**Eva Scanlan**

The production runs for approximately 60 minutes, with no interval.

AUTHOR'S NOTE

I'm fascinated by heartbreak. It's terrifying to fall so fully in love with someone that you feel you would die without them. The thought of losing them makes your knees buckle. You bargain with god – take my right arm, but don't take that person. That's how E feels about the cyclist. I wanted to capture the self sacrificing, undignified depths you sink to in the name of "love".

I recovered from an eating disorder. It defined a good decade of my life. As a result I am intrigued by people's coping mechanisms, the shame attached to them, and the lengths we go to to hide them from others. I wanted to explore self harm and addiction, but with an abstract spin on things. Hence the mustard.

When I was sick I put mustard on everything – toast, broccoli, eggs. It's low in calories, and I'd have spoons of it with every meal. Even now I'm still a bit obsessed with it. I suppose I called the main character E, because she is a strange other-worldly version of me.

When we first performed the show we used a mix of cheap hair conditioner and turmeric for the mustard. My skin was yellow for days. I looked genuinely ill. Later my stage manager came up with a more sophisticated concoction.

I wrote and rehearsed this tiny passion project in my house in London. Hildegard (my work wife) script edited, directed and designed the set and costumes. She had such a clear and striking vision for the piece. Winning a Fringe First at Edinburgh was a huge career highlight. I had no idea how it would be received but it turns out this play is small but mighty. Like a tiny jar of Colman's.

Eva O'Connor, June 2020

CREATIVE BIOS

EVA O'CONNOR is a writer and performer from Ogonnelloe Co. Clare. She trained at Rose Bruford drama school, and runs Sunday's Child theatre company with Hildegard Ryan. Her work has been produced in Ireland, the UK, France, Belgium, Australia, and the US. She has won multiple awards for her work, including a Scotsman Fringe First for *MUSTARD*, at the Edinburgh Fringe 2019.

HILDEGARD RYAN is a director in theatre and TV, hailing from Skerries co. Dublin. Hildegard studied English and History in Trinity College Dublin, and Film Production at CFS London. Her graduation short film was selected for the Cannes Film Festival short film corner in 2014.

Hildegard has collaborated with Eva O'Connor since 2013. She directed *My Name is Saoirse* (winner of First Fortnight Award at the Dublin Fringe 2014, the Argus Angel at the Brighton Fringe 2015, and the Best Theatre Award at the Adelaide Fringe 2017). She directed *Overshadowed* for the stage, and for its BBC Three screen adaptation. *Overshadowed* was nominated for a 2018 Rose d'Or Award and won the Mind Media Award for Best Drama in 2019.

With O'Connor, Hildegard has co-written and directed *The Friday Night Effect*, which debuted at the Edinburgh Fringe Festival 2017. She also directed O'Connor's *MUSTARD* which won a Fringe First and the Summerhall Lustrum award at the Edinburgh Fringe 2019.

Having directed a standalone episode for series 7, Hildegard has just wrapped on directing four episodes of *The Dumping Ground* series 8 for CBBC.

MARIANNE NIGHTINGALE is a lighting technician and designer from South East England. She studied Technical Theatre as part of an apprenticeship at Richmond Theatre, London.

Throughout her profession she has worked as part of the lighting department in multiple producing theatres on many successful productions: *The Inheritance, Ivan and the Dogs* (Young Vic Theatre); *My Name is Lucy Barton, A German Life* (The Bridge Theatre), Royal Court Theatre and The National Theatre.

Maz has been involved with Fishamble since 2018 and has been working with O'Connor & Ryan for more than 5 years on productions including: *My Name is Saoirse* (Best Theatre Award at the Adelaide Fringe 2017), *The Friday Night Effect, Maz and Bricks* and in 2019 was the lighting designer for O'Connor's *MUSTARD*.

JIM CULLETON is the artistic director of Fishamble: The New Play Company. He has directed many productions in Ireland and internationally, winning awards including an Olivier Award in 2016 for *Silent* by Pat Kinevane and the Irish Times Best Director Award in 2020 for *The Alternative* by Michael Patrick and Oisín Kearney. He has also directed for companies including the Abbey, Gaiety, RTÉ, as well as on Broadway and the West End.

GAVIN KOSTICK, as literary manager at Fishamble, works with new writers for theatre through script development, readings and a variety of mentorship programmes. For Fishamble Gavin is particularly proud of his work on *Show in a Bag, The New Play Clinic, Tiny Plays for Ireland* and *A Play for Ireland*. Gavin is also an award-winning playwright. He has written over twenty plays that have been produced nationally and internationally. Favourite works include: *Invitation to a Journey* and *The End of the Road* (Fishamble); *This is What we Sang for Kabosh, Fight Night, The Games People Play* and *At the Ford (RISE)* and the Libretto for *The Alma Fetish* (Raymond Deane and Wide Open Opera). As a performer he performed Joseph Conrad's *Heart of Darkness: Complete*, a six hour show for Absolut Fringe, Dublin Theatre Festival and The London Festival of Literature at the Southbank. His work in all areas has received many national and international awards.

EVA SCANLAN is the general manager and producer of Fishamble. Producing work includes: *On Blueberry Hill* by Sebastian Barry; *The Alternative* by Michael Patrick & Oisín Kearney; *Before* by Pat Kinevane; *Rathmines Road* by Deirdre Kinahan; *Haughey\Gregory* by Colin Murphy; Fishamble's award-winning Pat Kinevane Trilogy on tour in Ireland and internationally; *The Humours of Bandon* by Margaret McAuliffe; *Maz and Bricks* by Eva O'Connor; *Inside the GPO* by Colin Murphy; *Tiny Plays for Ireland* and *America and Swing* on tour in Ireland, the UK, and Australia. Eva produces *The 24 Hour Plays: Dublin* at the Abbey Theatre in Ireland

(2012-present), in association with the 24 Hour Play Company, New York, and has worked on *The 24 Hour Plays* on Broadway and *The 24 Hour Musicals* at the Gramercy Theatre. Previously, she was Producer of terraNOVA Collective in New York (2012-2015).

ABOUT SUNDAY'S CHILD

Sunday's Child is an award winning Irish theatre company run by Eva O'Connor and Hildegard Ryan. Their plays include: *My Name is Saoirse* (Winner of First Fortnight Award Dublin Fringe 2014, Argus Angel Award Brighton Fringe 2015, Best Theatre Award Adelaide Fringe 2017); *Overshadowed* (Winner of Fishamble Award for Best New Writing 2015 and now a series on BBC Three), *The Friday Night Effect*, and *MUSTARD*. Eva and Hildegard collaborate on work for stage, screen and radio.

Eva and Hildegard are delighted to be working with Fishamble on *MUSTARD*. Eva's play *Maz and Bricks* was directed by Olivier award-winning Jim Culleton, and produced by Fishamble, and she is thrilled to be collaborating with them again.

Eva would like to thank Jim Culleton, Eva Scanlan, Chandrika Narayanan-Mohan and Gavin Kostick for their unwavering support in developing and producing work. They are true champions of the arts.

Eva would also like to thank her literary agent Frances Arnold, from Rochelle Stevens & Co. for her brilliant work ethic and words of wisdom.

ABOUT FISHAMBLE

"Ireland's leading new writing company"
THE STAGE
Fishamble is passionate about discovering, developing and producing new plays. It is named after the Playhouse on Dublin's Fishamble Street which, in the 1780s, became the first theatre to commission and produce plays by Irish writers.

"Fishamble puts electricity in the National grid of dreams"
SEBASTIAN BARRY
Fishamble believes that vibrant theatre stands at the centre of a vibrant civic society. It harnesses the imaginative power of theatre to provide audiences with a diverse range of contemporary, compelling and heartfelt dramatic works.

"a global brand with international theatrical presence"
THE IRISH TIMES
Fishamble thinks nationally and reaches globally. It works collaboratively with networks of artists, communities, and organisations, to achieve the maximum possible life for its plays. For instance, over 30 Fishamble playscripts have been published.

Fishamble has toured its productions to audiences throughout Ireland, and to 19 other countries. It typically produces over 200 performances annually, from the Aran Islands to Auckland, Ballymun to Brisbane, Clonmel to Cleveland.

"forward-thinking Fishamble"
THE NEW YORK TIMES
Fishamble champions the role of the playwright, through its productions, and wide range of artist supports and development initiatives. It works with over 50% of the writers of all new plays produced on the island of Ireland each year.

"excellent Fishamble...Ireland's terrific Fishamble"
THE GUARDIAN
Fishamble has received many awards in Ireland and internationally, including an Olivier Award, won jointly with Pat Kinevane. Its living archive is at the National Library of Ireland.

"when Fishamble is [in New York], you've got to go"
TIME OUT NEW YORK

STAFF

Jim Culleton (Artistic Director)
Eva Scanlan (General Manager & Producer)
Gavin Kostick (Literary Manager)
Chandrika Narayanan-Mohan (Marketing & Development
Manager)
Ronan Carey (Office & Production Coordinator)

BOARD

Padraig Burns, Peter Finnegan, Louise Molloy, Doireann Ní
Bhriain (Chair), Vincent O'Doherty, John O'Donnell, Siobhan
O'Leary (Vice Chair), Andrew Parkes, Colleen Savage

FISHAMBLE'S RECENT AND CURRENT PRODUCTIONS

• *The Alternative* by Michael Patrick & Oisín Kearney (2019),
the chosen play from Fishamble's A PLAY FOR IRELAND
programme, touring in Ireland
• *On Blueberry Hill* by Sebastian Barry (2017–20) touring in
Ireland, Europe, Off-Broadway, Trafalgar Entertainment/West
End
• *Before* by Pat Kinevane (2018–20) touring in association with
the Strollers Network, and internationally
• *Haughey|Gregory* by Colin Murphy (2018–19) in the Abbey
Theatre, Mountjoy Prison, Dáil Éireann, Croke Park, and Larkin
Community College, as well as on national tour with the Nasc
Network
• *The Humours of Bandon* by Margaret McAuliffe (2017–20)
touring in Ireland, UK, US, and Australia
• *Rathmines Road* by Deirdre Kinahan (2018) in coproduction
with the Abbey Theatre
• *Drip Feed* by Karen Cogan (2018) in coproduction with Soho
Theatre, touring in Ireland and UK
• *GPO 1818* by Colin Murphy (2018) to mark the bicentenary of
the GPO
• *Maz & Bricks* by Eva O'Connor (2017–20) touring in Ireland,
UK, and Off-Broadway
• *Forgotten, Silent and Underneath* by Pat Kinevane (since 2007,
2011 and 2014, respectively –2020) touring in Ireland, UK,
Europe, US, Australia and New Zealand

- *Charolais* by Noni Stapleton (2017) in New York
- *Inside the GPO* by Colin Murphy (2016) performed in the GPO during Easter
- *Tiny Plays for Ireland and America* by 26 writers (2016) at the Kennedy Center, Washington DC, and Irish Arts Center, New York, as part of Ireland 100
- *Mainstream* by Rosaleen McDonagh (2016) in coproduction with Project Arts Centre
- *Invitation to a Journey* by David Bolger, Deirdre Gribbin and Gavin Kostick (2016) in coproduction with CoisCéim, Crash Ensemble, and Galway International Arts Festival
- *Little Thing, Big Thing* by Donal O'Kelly (2014–16) touring in Ireland, UK, Europe, US and Australia
- *Swing* by Steve Blount, Peter Daly, Gavin Kostick and Janet Moran (2014–16) touring in Ireland, UK, Europe, US, Australia and New Zealand
- *Spinning* by Deirdre Kinahan (2014) at Dublin Theatre Festival
- *The Wheelchair on My Face* by Sonya Kelly (2013–14) touring in Ireland, UK, Europe and US.

SUPPORT DARING NEW PLAYWRITING AND FEARLESS VOICES

Support Fishamble's work by becoming a Friend, making a donation, or encouraging your company to support Fishamble.

Become a Friend of Fishamble today by scanning the QR code below, or visiting www.fishamble.com/become-a-friend

To find out all the ways in which you can support Fishamble, visit **fishamble.com/support-us** or contact Chandrika Narayanan-Mohan on **+353 (0)1 6704018.**

We wish to thank the following Friends for their invaluable support:
Alan & Rosemary Ashe, ATM Accounting Services, Mary Banotti, Tania Banotti, Doireann Ní Bhriain, Conor Braiden, Colette and Barry Breen, Business to Arts, Claudia Carroll, Sandra Carroll, Breda Cashe, Maura Connolly, John & Yvonne Healy, Gillie Hinds, Robert Gilligan, Jane Majeski, Monica McInerney, Stuart Mclaughlin, Ger McNaughton, Sinead Moriarty, Pat Moylan, Dympna Murray, Liz Nugent, Lisney, Tom O'Connor, Vincent O'Doherty, Siobhan O'Leary, Nora Owen, Andy Pollak, David & Veronica Rowe, Jennifer Russell, Colleen Savage, Mary Stephenson, Patrick Sutton, and Tesco Finest. We thank all those who contributed generously and wish to remain anonymous.

Fishamble is a registered charity no. CHY 20103958.
Fishamble is funded by the Arts Council, Dublin City Council, and Culture Ireland.

fishamble.com
facebook.com/fishamble
twitter.com/fishamble

Acknowledgements
Thanks to the following for their help with this production: Rachel West and all at the Arts Council; Ray Yeates and all at Dublin City Council Arts Office; Christine Sisk, Ciaran Walsh, Valerie Behan and all at Culture Ireland; Laura MacNaughton, Aoife McCollum and all at the O'Reilly Theatre; all at 3 Great Denmark Street; Frances Arnold; all those who have helped since this publication went to print.

To my mum, the most creative woman I know.
I love you Ange. X

CHARACTERS

E

Mustard:
A thing of yellow.
Pasty.
Strong, by name and nature.
The only British import in our home.
With sausages, bread, broccoli even.
Taytos dipped in.
Mum's crisps and Colman's sandwiches
on a Friday night in.
I well remember
the first smear on skin.
The pure pain of it.
The glass jar used sparingly shame of it.
Scars screaming.
Wounds alight.
So wrong,
yet so yellowy right.

We have sex.
Good hard satisfying sex.
Solid sex.
Sex that hurts in all the right places.
Sex at angles that feel
slightly dangerous
for my internal organs.
Sex that makes me teeter
on the borders of pain.
Rough sex,
I suppose you could call it.

Sex that makes me bleed.

Sex that makes sense.

Sex that doesn't require an instruction manual.

Sex that makes me cry.

Sex that is over quite fast.

Sex that doesn't make me come.

Which is fine.

It's possibly even a good thing

because realistically

I don't think that kind of intensity

would be good for either of us.

At this time.

And besides, tonight isn't about pleasure

or being taken to higher places,

or feeling safe,

or being valued.

It's about getting fucked.

And I've ticked that box.

And it's about getting back together.

And I'm gonna tick that box very hard,

very soon.

I can feel it in the walls of my tired vagina.

It's a year on.

A collection of months,

stacked like volumes of encyclopedias,

propping each other up,

gathering dust
but otherwise,
redundant.

A year of pain
in the crevices of my elbows,
at the backs of my knees,
behind my eyes,
in corners of me I didn't know existed.

A year of struggle
and screech.
Of nails yanked out of finger beds.
Of grieving.
Worse than a bereavement
I read somewhere once.
At least in death
there is a grave
to piss and spit and cry on.
A year of mustard.
Hot, sharp, yellow, pasty, shameful.

A year seemed like a decent,
if arbitrary length of time
to get my shit together.
On the anniversary
The Blessed Virgin Mary would appear to me
and wipe my mind and muscle memory.
Delete the contents of me.
I'd be like an old computer
getting rebooted to fuck

by Jesus's merciful ma.

On the anniversary

I'd wake up,

wounds healed.

All traces of him –

the taste of the inside of his mouth,

the sound of him on steps,

his concentration face,

the smell of him sleeping –

would be just like that

puff of smoke

gonezo.

On the anniversary

My mind would not go to mustard.

Eleven months three weeks and one day on.

It's the dead of night.

I'm couch slouching.

Thinking about sex.

Lack thereof.

Vagina closed for business.

Even a bean flick feels like

a betrayal.

When he calls me.

The letters, numbers that make him up

flash on my phone screen.

They trigger something

in my head.

A high.

Like a hefty key of coke
up my nose.
I fumble and panic answer.
I'm afraid to blink or breathe.
His voice is like warm water.
Like everything good coming back to me.
Eleven months three weeks and one day
since we spoke.
"Hey. It would be good to see you."
Just like that he summons me.
Back into his life.
Back into his bed.
From the depths of rural Ireland
I buy a Ryanair flight.
Click click click.
The internet is tutting me.
Thirty nine ninety nine one way.
Bus bus train plane bus schlep.
Cross counties.
Cross countries.
I think I might wet myself
with the ecstasy of another chance.
My mind goes to mustard.

Less than twenty four hours since the summons
I am doorstepping him.
The Crouch End Castle looms above.
And then him.
The shape of him.

A stranger now, and yet relentlessly familiar.

My home.

"Come in and up," he says.

A year since I last graced his bed.

His memory foam mattress has forgotten me.

I am a foreign object.

I press my shoulder blades,

my ankle bones,

the round of my ass

into the soft of it.

The mattress yields to me.

Him less so.

Tonight he will pop the question.

He will sit bolt upright

against his non-existent headboard,

lean his naked sinewy back

against the yellow wallpaper,

he will hold my face in his hands,

like it's made of precious stone,

and say something along the lines of:

"E Remember those flesh coloured granny pants you left on
my banisters the night you walked out. The night I forced
you to walk out? I have washed, dried, ironed and folded
them and they are in my top drawer. *Our* top drawer. Will
you move back in with me?"

Except he is slow with the question.

For now there is only silence.

And the silence is the weight of concrete.

We lie beside each other like formal old people,

drowning in it.
A small bit of our shoulder skin is touching,
maybe one square inch.
Sweaty,
laced with sex juice.
Like a skinny layer of cling film.
"There is sex juice on our shared shoulder,"
I want to say to him.
Maybe that would undrown us
from our concrete silence.
But I don't.
Because if there's one thing
I know he likes,
it is when I hold my tongue.

One year previously.
We met on a night out
in Elephant and Castle
so hip it physically hurt.
I was truly madly deeply unhappy that night,
surrounded by girls
who looked like emaciated teenagers
direct from the nineties,
and boys
in pearly white socks
and pearly white teeth,
all matchy matchy
under the glowing UV lights.
Picture this:

I'm queuing for a drink

when I recognise a Greek lad,

Jorgos

behind the bar.

He is tall,

emaciated with dreads

and a look in his sunken eyes

that says

"Austerity fucked my country and Angela Merkel can suck
the dick of my mother."

I had a disastrous one night stand

with Jorgos

a while back,

which ended in tears

when I refused to have anal sex with him

in front of a full-length mirror.

"Jorgos, Jorgos hey!"

I'm waving at him, drowning waving.

It's pretty clear he doesn't fancy a chat

but I'm in full self-destruct mode.

"Jorgos! How are things in the...warehouse?"

"We were evicted," he says. "What do you want to drink?"

I order a vodka

and sugar-free tropical Red Bull

and with a single twitch

of his left eyebrow

he makes it clear,

(just incase he hadn't before)

that he thinks I'm trash.

I am trash.

My mind goes to mustard.

I lock myself

in a flooded bathroom cubicle.

Squelch squelch,

bang bang

"Can you hurry up in there love there's a fucking queue!"

I find a baggie in a sanitary bin,

tucked in beside a bloodied

snickers wrapper.

It's MDMA.

Sweet Molly Malone.

I tip and swallow the crystals

in one go.

I gag and wince

and slip sheepish from the cubicle.

A gaggle of impatient girls

swan in after me.

"Smells like come up shit in here."

I wander lonely as a cloud

through dry ice

and damp corridors.

I pass bodies of bodies

of shiny happy party people.

I'm coming up now,

from whatever it was I took.

Coming up at the speed of a glass elevator,

at the speed of *swooosh*

when it dawns on me...

this shit could be rat poison.

The absolute fear

swims in my veins.

Could be rat poison cut with concrete.

Everything's cut with concrete these days.

And then a wave of who gives a fuck.

Sure if it's the end

it's the end.

I make a beeline for the smoking area

in search of a stick of lung cancer,

my heart fluttering,

the Molly in me

like rocket fuel.

Or rat poison.

In mushrooms of smoke

I slide down against wire fencing

and press up against it

'til I've diamond marks

on my flesh.

I stare at the ankles of strangers.

A sea of mustard socks

and Nike Air Max.

Someone slides down beside me.

A body of heat.

Looks at me.

He is stunning this boy beside me.

I am sick with it.

His freckled skin

is the most perfect organ

I have beheld in my sight.

His eyes are the green of cats.

Swimming pools of intrigue.

His calves catch my eye,

chiseled, and bulging in his jeans,

like strange angry fruits.

It occurs to me that I am chewing my face.

Hashtag no regrets.

"Do you have a fag I could tap?"

"I don't smoke."

"Neither do I."

He smiles at me with a laugh in his eyes and I am melting.

On the dancefloor,

hemmed in,

a sea of sweat and skin.

I'm up only to his broad chest.

Eye level at his nipples.

I see them just

through the thin fabric of his t-shirt

the colour of shark.

The heat off him,

like home to me.

Molecules shifting and drifting

and then really fucking shifting.

My wet mouth on his,

grinning through the kiss.

Eu-pho-ri-a.

Break apart sharpish and praise the DJ.

All hail the fucking DJ.
Where uuunnce uuuunnnce
is concerned
touchy feely is frowned upon.
Worship the gods of techno,
not the body of the man next to you.
Them's the rules.
I steal delicious glances at him.
My smoking area man.
My loneliness gone.
Banished.
Not a trace of mustard in my mind.

Later a bouncer winks at us.
He unclips a VIP cordon and
ushers us upstairs
to a crusty office-cum-broom cupboard.
Inside there are bodies
strewn across every surface,
lolling, lounging,
horsing through fags.
Someone tosses me an ice-cold Red Stripe
and I gulp it down
like Jesus in the desert
on the last day of Lent.
Smoking area man
plants a hot and tickly whisper
in my ear.
"Welcome to the green room."

The déjà vu of it floors me.

Have we been here before? I want to ask.

But instead I say

"The green room? But the walls are grey."

We take to a swivel chair.

Round and round the bend he spins me.

I'm curled cat like.

Foetal and full on,

soul spilling him my story.

Telling him that my friends,

while not bad people *per se*,

were either too drunk or too bored

to deal with me in my present condition.

My tongue is loose now,

oily as fuck.

The word vomit betrays me.

Jorgos appears in the doorway.

Darkens it.

He looks at me like I'm seven headed.

"What's she doing in here?"

Smoking area man slips his arm

tighter still around my waist,

eyeballs Jorgos

and announces:

"She's with us. She's with me."

And I am.

Later we dance around

the death trap

that is Elephant and Castle roundabout,

light limbed and giddy.

We are hungry for each other.

We skip past the half-dismantled shopping centre,

a shrine to threading shops

and Polish supermarkets.

It's just us,

and people work and church bound.

Colourful, pressed, sickeningly fresh.

On we go up toward the scummy Thames.

Sorry "Tems" hard for us Irish.

Always "tee-hayches" in the wrong place.

Or worse still

none at all.

Turty tree and a turd.

He slags me.

I call him an evil coloniser.

We talk about life and love and London.

We talk with frankness that lasts

for that delicious window of time,

when everything between you and a stranger

is good

and unblemished.

When there are no secrets, or raised guards, or impulses to lie.

When we arrive at his castle in Crouch End,

I loiter on the doorstep

and behold it with suspicion.

Where is the buzzer

for his apartment

contained within this vast dollhouse?

This obnoxious stately home.

"My parents aren't using it. They live in the South of France now."

He says this without a grain of embarrassment,

as he turns the key in the door.

Click.

He has in his possession an unflinching certainty of himself.

A thing that comes with Englishness.

Like mustard.

The Crouch End Castle is old,

three floors steep,

stairs deep and uneven

that would trip and flounder even

that surest of mountain goats.

Bikes old and new

dangle from the ceiling

like delicate floating spaceships.

An elaborate modern art exhibition,

hung drawn and seldom used.

More money above my head

than I've ever seen in my life.

"I'm a professional cyclist," he explains.

"Like Tour de France Lance Armstrong professional cyclist? Like team Sky doped up to the nines professional cyclist?"

He laughs. Something like that.

I reach up and spin a wheel.

I see my fortune whir in mid air.

He snatches my wrist.

"Don't."

He tells me cycling saved his life.

His eyes glint with freedom, just at the mention of it.

I can see him in my mind's eye:

streaking into the horizon

on a skinny frame,

wind in his hair.

Eating the future,

like a bullet.

He speaks about cycling

the way my mother speaks about Jesus

and her evangelic church-cult community

in rural Ireland.

The one with only six members

that meets in a room

above SuperValu on a Sunday morning

to sip consecrated Ribena

from stained Sports Direct mugs,

and sing praise songs

such as *"Fly Jesus Fly"*.

It was his grandad who got him into cycling.

It's a privilege

he tells me.

To race in his tracks.

To tear up the roads in his wake.

To know that someone you love has gone before you.

It makes every uphill struggle worth it.

"And what about you?"

What about me?

"What makes you tick?"

I tell him what I can.

Ireland to London.

The struggle is real.

An artist I say.

Once was.

Or hoped to make a stab at.

Fresh off the boat

with a suitcase full of dreams.

A clueless Irish girl

with a pocketful of kindle.

Twigs and sticks

gathered from the damp earth

of the back arse of nowhere.

Hungry, desperate to start a fire.

But for whatever reason,

probably the wet of my tears

or the damp of the bog,

the fire never took.

I shrug, the way Irish people do.

I am ok, I assure him.

I am figuring it out.

Finding other ways to stay alive.

"There's something about you," he says.

He takes my face in his hands

like it's made of precious stone.

"Fuck the damp of the bog. There's a spark. There's a fire in you."

He's right.

Inside I'm burning.

My mind goes to mustard.

From there

things move at the speed

of a doped-up cycling team

free wheeling down the Alps

on the last stage of the Tour De France.

I learn him like a language I was thirsty for,

that might de-code the world for me.

I learn him by heart.

His forearms strong and veiny,

rammed full of just the right amount

of muscle, bone and sinew.

His calves carved from stone.

His scar;

raw pink and raised up

between his rib cage,

the colour of smoked salmon.

It is genuinely erotic to the touch.

It goes like this:

cancel everything and ride each other silly.

Nights spent going hard at it,

days spent in lazy recovery,

thighs in bits,

mind splintered

into a thousand blissed out pieces.

Those days are the lick of salty skin,

the trace of collar bones,
the wet of kisses you might drown in.
Those days are higher places
and lucky stars
and I count my moons,
and text my evangelic mother
to tell her the Lord is smiling on me.

The good times are good.
They are crazy manic good.
Being with him is like being on steroids.
Thrilling, torturous, addictive.
There is something spiritual about his smell.
Things jigsaw click into place.
After years of grinding themselves to dust
the cogs of my life align.
They sync and circle
and click.
I dream I can usurp the bikes,
that I can pedestal myself.
Eclipse even cycling in the ranks.
But quick and sharpish
the penny drops.
I will always came second to skinny frames,
to wheels so slight
when they spin
they are barely even there.
Quick and sharpish I learn that cycling is his God,
training his religion,

and Lance Armstrong was wrong
when he said it's not about the bike –
because it is.
Completely.
I move in with the cyclist into the Crouch End Castle.
There's no down on one knee
move in proposal.
No specially cut key in a ribboned box.
No feet swept from under me.
No "I'll carry you over the threshold".
No "I'll drink to you my live-in love".
More of a slip slide into since you're here you might as well stay.
One day I do not leave the castle
and he does not ask me why.
This I take for love.

I stop talking to my mum.
I clean cut her out of my life.
My silence a sweet and strange relief
for her,
I am sure.
Her pesky dependent
has finally unlatched, unleeched.
I no longer call her in the dead of night.
With unhealthy urgency
with breath caught in throat,
with pleas for prayers
with
"Mum

I don't think I can
Mum the thing is
the mustard is..."
Come to me all you who are weary and I shall give you rest.
I whisper sometimes
when the hot and panicky of missing her
slips its fingers round my neck.
But otherwise
I revel in the fact
that I have outgrown my mother.
I have outgrown even mustard.
I catch myself in every shiny surface
and double take.
I behold myself and marvel.
I am functional as fuck.

The cyclist trains more
and looks at me less.
His eyes the green of cats
no longer swim with intrigue at the sight of me.
One day I confront him,
beg him to hold my face in his hands
like it's made of precious stone.
To look and really see me.
He stares me down for long enough
to ask me
have I always floundered like this,
have I always grappled desperately for direction?
Have I always thieved oxygen from the lungs of others

until they too
have trouble breathing?
He says this
matter-of-factly.
Words choice and crisp
dripping in poison.
As he backs a bike out the door
careful not to clip the pedals
against the wall,
careful to protect what matters most.

My mind goes to mustard.
It blurs my vision,
smothers me in my sleep,
I dream of it
on my skin.
The searing yellowy pain of it.
The shame of it.
Physically I avoid it.
I walk the line.
Tightroping
through supermarkets
like an alcoholic
playing at being good.
Flirting, skirting the booze lane.
Beetle scurrying home to safety.
The cyclist knows nothing
of the madness in my bones
or the mustard in my mind.

I think I might burst with it.

Smear the walls of the Crouch End Castle

in thickest Colman's,

in dirty protest.

Perhaps then the intrigue might return

to his cat green eyes?

The cyclist is perpetually away.

A loyal slave

to all day all night,

all consuming

training.

Relentless competitions.

He's leaving for a month this time –

the longest stint yet.

"I could go with you for support?"

I offer.

"I could accompany you to far flung corners of the cycling universe? I could stadium stand, and sideline whistle as you whiz in circles on indoor racetracks mounted on your one true love, the fucking bicycle. I could cheer and shriek and lay down my body at the finish line?"

"No need." he says,

"Easier to focus when I'm on my own."

So I mind the house.

I doggedly babysit the Crouch End Castle.

I pad up and down

the spiteful steps

that trip me still.

I hang my beige coloured granny pants

(the Sloggi ones he hates)

from his banisters to dry.

I rattle around

in my palace of angst.

Time spent with myself

feeling less and less safe.

I hawk like stalk him online.

His face beams out at me

high on the win.

His skin is still the most perfect organ

I have beheld in my sight.

His muscles, the very ones I have traced

with awestruck fingers,

are glinting with sweat and victory.

He hasn't messaged me.

His radio silence a noose around my neck.

I lie with my phone

bargaining with Jesus until:

a text.

My stomach flips.

From my mother.

"Praying for you pet."

I picture her

giving me up to the Lord

over consecrated Ribena

of a Sunday.

Hands clasped with her cultish comrades.

Tasteless body of Christ wafers freshly dissolved.

As they pray in tongues

for me to be saved.

I fantasise about
the high of his return.
How he will relent.
Let me collapse
into the lean of him.
He will kiss me full force on the mouth.
Eu-pho-ri-a.
This thing,
this love,
is like steroids.
Thrilling, torturous, addictive.
It will kill me.
I go to bed night after night
with madness in my bones,
with mustard on my mind.
All I want is to writhe around in yellow,
'til my organs feel the heat.
'til they sear,
and melt
and fail me.
Then one 4am.
The click of the front door.
I upright bolt in the bed.
Spine tingly against the non-existent headboard.
I listen to the quiet shuffle of feet
easing the trophy bike
into the hallway.
Careful not to clip the pedals against the wall.
I scuttle to the banisters.

I drape myself over.

I down peer

to behold the head of the man

I love so much.

Returned to me.

The relief like

morphine

in my veins.

It is then I see a second head.

Blond and scraped back.

A laugh,

giddy, light, flirtatious,

meets my ears.

A "sshhhh".

A "c'min to the kitchen".

I am

as I descend the stairs two at a time,

a silent, surefooted

mountain goat.

The spiteful stairs don't trip me now.

Outside the kitchen door

I ear press

and keyhole peer.

I breath hold

and pray to Jesus.

My insides

are those of

a gutted fish.

I am sick

with the scraped backed blond
of her.

With the treachery of him.

He pours her a hefty glass of red

and it's all

stained teeth

and cycling chat.

It's all training this

and protein that.

She is built of lean like him.

Her edges are angular.

Her calves too are carved from stone.

I feel dumpy, useless, soft.

He takes her face in his hands

like it's made of precious stone.

She laughs.

He "sshhhhes" her again.

This time with a kiss.

My mind goes to mustard.

My local Turkish shop only has a handful of jars

next to the hummus on the shelves.

Two pounds a jar

steep enough,

but I'm in no fit state to bargain.

I smile excuses over the counter

at the nice Turkish man's raised eyebrows.

Bushy and obscenely long.

"Baking," I say as I hand over cash.

As I clean them out of house and home.

Then up the road to Morrisons.

A trolley load there,

glass clinking on glass.

My heart fluttering with the rush of it.

A better high than the mandy in the bin.

Morrisons woman on the till

is bored to tears.

Thank god.

Doesn't bat a singular eyelid

as she beeps them through.

Her disinterest is a sweet relief.

Lidl next.

Should have gone there first really.

Ninety-eight pence a jar

fair fucks to the Germans.

Vielen dank then out the door.

Then I pass a Tesco,

a shite Metro one,

but might as well pop in.

Would be rude not to.

Every Little Helps.

Can barely walk under the weight

of three baskets full.

Arms yanked out of sockets.

The looks I get on the bus

as I homeward trek

to assess the haul.

I decide I need more

to be safe.

So onto Amazon Prime I go.

Fingers dancing over keyboard in anticipation.

One hundred jars.

Same day delivery please.

Clean out my account.

At this point

Fuck it.

I am frantic

with the thrill

of giving in.

*E opens multiple jars of mustard. She slathers it slowly
and deliberately all over skin until she is completely yellow
and burning. It is excruciating.*

When he comes home

I am surrounded.

I am ear height.

I am skin deep.

I am up to my neck in it.

His lip twitches

as he struggles to compute

the yellow fuckery before his eyes

"What's this?" he manages eventually.

"MUSTARD." I say.

"Obviously. English mustard. Pure and strong and brilliant.
Much like yourself."

His eyes are dancing with disgust

but he can't take them off me.

I can go now he says.

I can take myself,

my mess,

my junk,

my beige coloured granny pants,

my bullshit,

my my my

mustard

(he can barely say the word)

and be gone.

I can rinse myself out

and smash myself

into the nearest recycling bin.

I can slather and smooth and paste

and die

for all he cares.

There will be no mustard

on the Crouch End carpet!

Not on his watch!

My mouth is watering

with the shame of it –

of ever thinking

he could cure me

of the madness in my bones,

the mustard in my mind.

I look down at my yellow limbs.

There are better ways to survive.

This I know.

I could set him alight,

take a match to his perfect skin.

I could torch his fucking castle to the ground.

But it's myself I want to burn.

When you've nothing left to lose

you have to set yourself on fire.

My mother arrives

to whisk me home

to rural Ireland.

She is dressed head to foot

in a lilac ski suit.

It's lavender she corrects me.

I behold her, in all her eccentric glory.

She opens her mouth,

to pray for me,

I'm sure.

But instead she says

"Oh pet. You're not well. Your heart is hurt."

The view is, on paper, breathtaking.

Roll and tumbling hills,

patchwork fields.

Lough Derg is glassy and mirage-like,

so tranquil it's infuriating.

"Drink that in. A lake full of a calm."

Says mum, as we step out of her banged up Ford Fiesta,

the same two-door tin can

of social humiliation

I hid in the back seat of

when I was seven.

I stare at the lake with blank in my eyes.

I am behind a pane of glass.

Pain in every crevice of me,

in corners of me I didn't know existed.

I want to fold over and in on myself.

Like bread mix.

Mum shites on about nothing in particular.

She has to go out tonight.

To her Christian ladies sewing class.

She hopes I don't mind.

"You'll be good now, when I'm gone. You'll be grand."

She says willing me to be.

I'm hollow and quiet.

I thank her.

For whisking me home,

for bearing the weight of me.

I wonder what she will tell them about me,

the holy stitchers and bitchers.

The truth I'm sure.

That I have no one

and nothing.

That I am sick.

That the cyclist had no more use for me.

That I mean well

but my mind goes to mustard.

"I'd skip the sewing," she says.

"But Maureen's husband is after getting arrested for smuggling phones into Limerick prison. And him a garda himself. So I should probably go down and help her with her patchwork quilt."

I lie on my single bed
and ceiling stare at plastic stars.
I think of the cyclist
and his new squeeze
in all her angular edges.
I think of the shared glug of generous red.
I can feel the good glass beneath her lips.
The thin of it.
I will it to shatter.
I will it to slice open her mouth
'till it's torn and red and bloody.

I have two hours 'til mum is home from sewing.
I am a zombie in my own skin.
I can feel the tip of the scales
into madness.
Every inch of me is screaming for it.
I am addled
with an insatiable hunger for mustard.
I set off out the gate and down the lane
at the speed of trot.
I know the roads
off by the palm of my heart.
Winding hairpin bends,
a strip of green up the middle,
the hedge past John Joe's farm
shaped like Stalin's head.
The local shop is how I remember it.
Understocked.

The shelves fuller with dead space

than actual items.

Fruit with skin leathery and loose.

Ann O'Driscoll behind the counter.

Time warped.

Shoulders dusted with dandruff.

Like someone smashed a snow globe over her head.

"Well well well," she says.

A smug sideways smile on her.

"And how are things in Landan?"

I buy as many jars as I can carry

"You're a fan of the mustard are ye?"

I schlep home quicker this time,

at the speed most humanly possible.

I have never been so desperate

for the searing yellow pain of it,

the shame of it.

I want to burn the skin off my bones.

I want to writhe around in yellow

'til even my organs feel the heat.

'Til they sear and melt and fail me.

"Are you trying to kill yourself with that stuff?"

Demands mum on her return.

Tears well in her eyes

when she catches me yellow handed in the act.

"No," I tell her. "I am trying to stay alive."

Cold turkey.

Cold sweats.

The yellow stuff is just like that

puff of smoke

gonezo.

Every surface,

every shelf in the house,

decolonised

of mustard.

My limbs cry out to be soothed.

To be smothered.

I am bereft.

I am heartbroken.

I have nothing now.

My mother refuses to give up on me.

She plies me with soup,

with soda bread,

with sugary tea.

She prays for me relentlessly.

A steady stream of Post-it notes

follows me around.

They are scrawled with bible verses:

*Do not worry about anything, but in everything, through prayer
and petition with thanksgiving, present your requests to God.
And the peace of God, which surpasses all understanding, will
guard your hearts and minds in Christ Jesus.*

I tear them down.

I scrunch and ball them

into the nearest bin.

I spit and screech

that I do not beleive in her God,

that she will never know a pain like this.

She tells me I am stronger

than mustard and men.

We are in the kitchen.

Mum is making bread,

the dough

like flesh,

bouncy and rebellious

beneath her expert fingers.

I am draped over the warm lid of the AGA,

head sideways to observe the kneading.

Suddenly I am a child again.

Content, hypnotised.

She pauses,

her fingers suspended in air and dough.

She is going to ask me something.

I can tell by the silence.

She is choosing her words, grappling for them.

"Which do you miss more? Him or... or... or?"

"Or what mum?"

"Or MUSTARD?" I offer. "Fuck you!"

I leave her kneading and stung.

I feel the hurt radiating from her

like the heat from the AGA.

I hate her for it.

Time passes.

Crawls by

on bloodied knees

and gravel encrusted palms.

The months heave themselves

one after the other

closer to the end of the world.

The cyclist will not speak to me.

I am blocked on every medium.

I am cancelled.

I call him repeatedly, relentlessly,

from rural Ireland.

His radio silence is a noose around my neck.

I tell myself it's the bad signal.

Or perhaps he's had a stroke while out on the bike.

My mind goes to mustard.

He wins a race.

A European title thing.

All headlines and gold medals.

A bright-as-the-sun career ahead.

I seize my opportunity with both hands

and email him

(the only medium not road blocked to me).

I painstakingly arrange the words:

Casual congratulations!

All the training paid off!

HUGE

ACHIEVEMENT.

Even made the Irish News.

Grandad would be proud.

Crazy how time flies.

Dot dot dot.

Between my carefully composed lines

I weave in

a guarantee.

A swear to God.

I Morse code in a message:

The way I was before.

I am different now.

I am not the same.

Please.

Days later he replies.

To tell me

he is changing his email address.

But he wishes me well.

He really does.

My mind goes to mustard.

On relapse number one hundred

and I couldn't even tell you what,

my mother pins me physically

to the wall of the utility room.

Her fingers death grip around my wrists.

She tile slams me,

between the microwave and washing machine,

into silence.

I am toe to head in yellow.

"STOP THIS! STOP THIS! WHY CAN'T YOU

STOP THIS?!!"

Her eyes are alive

and dancing

with the pain of everything

I have inflicted on her.

Her hands are yellowed now,

she too is contaminated.

She crumples then,

down on knees and bended hands.

Begging Jesus for strength and guidance.

Begging, begging, begging.

Mum is not keen on housebound.

There is a limit to the mope and sulk

that she can hack.

She gives me an ultimatum:

"Come to sewing with me of a Wednesday, or up sticks and vamoose."

We both know her threat is empty.

Hollow.

But I have no legs to stand on.

Mum arms me with a cross-stitch

I've been working on

since I was twelve.

Circle framed, greying, frayed at the edges.

It features

two blocky figurines

of me and mum

(a strange pair in real life

and in cross-stitch)

standing beside a half-stitched tree.

Christian Ladies stitch and bitch

is held in the local community hall.

There is mould crawling up the walls

the like of which would make your lungs black
just by looking.
But the "wimmin" don't seem to mind.
They sew at tiny infant tables,
miniature and wooden,
left over from when the place
was a primary school
sometime in the sixties.
I sit with Susan Silva
(from Thurles but married to a Brazilian)
Susan has wiry hair,
in fifty shades of grey.
She wears floor-length cardigans
and turquoise rings.
She has a certain sadness in her eyes.
She says little to me
as she knits one purls one,
knits one purls one,
and for that
gratitude oozes out my pores.
I wonder if
my mum has told her
about my troubles
with mustard and men.
At the end of the session
she smiles at me.
"Maybe see you next week?"
Her voice is thin like crepe paper.
Fat chance Susan, I think.

My mind goes to mustard.

But like a sulky tail between legs teenager
I attend Wednesday stitch and bitch,
religiously.
Wednesdays punctuate my week
with single hours of almost relief.
There is a kind of peace
in sitting with wiry-haired Susan Silva,
as she knits one purls one,
knits one purls one.
My cross-stitch is coming on.
My tree is nearly fully fledged.
It is growing some leaves.
"I like Susan," I grudgingly admit
to mum one day
in the tin can Ford Fiesta.
"Susan hasn't had it easy," mum tells me.
"Her Brazilian husband upped sticks and left her. Traded her
in for a younger, sunnier model. A year ago now. She still
goes by his name Silva, which is strange. Must be easier for
post and that."

Next Wednesday
one of the mouthy wimmen
at sewing
mentions cycling,
in passing.

"A mad sport so it is! Fierce exciting altogether! The Tour
de France is the perfect thing to watch as you rip back and
forward stitch and mend and darn and embroider!"

In my mind's eye

I see only yellow.

I glance down

at my underwhelming

cross-stitch.

I am paralysed

with pointlessness.

Susan stops her intricate

knit one purl one,

knit one purl one

and places her hand

on mine.

Her touch is as delicate as her crepe paper voice.

Tears spring me by surprise

and pool under my eyes.

"Maybe you should try swimming. For the sadness. The water
helped me with heartbreak."

The next day I go down to the lake.

It is, as usual,

glassy and mirage-like,

infuriatingly calm.

I strip down to

my beige coloured granny pants

for all the world to see.

I sick swallow

and shake my head

at Susan Silva
and her notions.

I launch myself from the pier,
all flailing limbs and echoey screech,
full force
into baltic Lough Derg.

The cold of it winds me,
shrinks my brain
and stuns my vagina.

I choke swallow a gulp of lake water.

Drink that in, a lake full of calm.

I can hear my mother's voice
as I flip
and float
and sky stare.

Euphoric
and freezing.

I scrabble back ashore.

I nod to a rat
that scampers up the rocks
beside me.

He is slithery and more nimble than me.

My skin is prickly
with exhilaration.

My mind goes
a little less
to mustard.

We lie beside each other
like formal old people,
drowning in silence.
A small bit of our shoulder skin
is touching.
Maybe one square inch.
It's sweaty,
laced with sex juice,
like a skinny layer of cling film.
He is staggeringly beautiful this boy beside me.
I am sick with it.
I am staggering backward
through time and space.
I am coming undone.
I am unraveling.
I am ready to give it all up
for one full kiss on the mouth.
I want him to look at me.
I want him to hold my face in his hands
like it's made of precious stone.
The silence is the weight of concrete.
He opens his mouth.
Fish like.
To say something.
The question.
The burning, burning question.
The heat of it
on my skin
like mustard.

"Listen. Seeing you has been. Great. You're great. But listen. The thing is. How can I. I'm not sure I'm gonna be able to sleep. With you here. Lying here. It's not. I think it's better if you. Leave."

Be. Gone.

He turns away from me.

I stare, stunned,

at his back.

The spine I know

off by the palm of my heart.

Which vertebra stack on top of which.

I reach out to touch it one last time

and he flinches.

He physically flinches.

Something in me snaps.

I slip out of the bed,

out of the room.

I pad down two flights of stairs,

a silent, surefooted

mountain goat.

The spiteful stairs don't trip me now.

I put my hand on my chest.

My soul is still inside,

screaming, but intact.

In the hallway

I pass under the vast array of bikes.

They dangle from the ceiling

like floating spaceships.

I pause under his favourite,

his baby, his German vintage racer.

It was his grandad's once.
It's so light I could almost lift it down with one hand.
I don't. I use two.
I hoist it down with great care and reverence
– it is after all a family heirloom.
The bike is too big for me,
too skinny.
I struggle to find my balance.
It feels like riding a flighty racehorse
made of air.
But the roads are quiet
and it is downhill
from his Crouch End Castle.
As I freewheel into the future on his German racer,
I remember that first night
he told me cycling saved his life.
I smile, because I know what he means now.
I think maybe cycling saved my life too.

By the time I get to the canal,
my eyes are streaming from the cold,
from the shock, from the flinch.
There's a single goose loitering
on the banks of the canal,
elegant and bored
as she potters
between the neat row of canal boats.
Lucy Goosey I'll call her.
She blinks at me blankly.

"Lucy I think I'm mad, I am mad, I am mad, I have never
felt so mad!"
There is no judgment
in her glassy eyes
as she watches me
fuck his German racer
full force into the canal.
Together we watch it
bob and sink and drown
as I once drowned
in his silence
the weight of concrete.

I wait for it.
For the hot and prickly panic
to spread over me like fire.
For the craving to swallow me.
But I feel strangely calm.
Lucy and I watch the ripply canal.
It is murky and disturbed.
"The water helped me with heartbreak." I tell her.

END

ABOUT THE AUTHOR

Eva O'Connor is a writer and performer from Ogonnelloe, Co. Clare. She studied English and German at Edinburgh University before completing an MA in theatre ensemble from Rose Bruford drama school in London.

Her plays include *My Best Friend Drowned in a Swimming Pool*, *Kiss Me and You Will See How Important I Am*, *My Name is Saoirse*, *Overshadowed*, *The Friday Night Effect* (co-written with Hildegard Ryan), *Maz and Bricks*, and *Mustard* (Fringe First winner 2019, the Summerhall Lustrum Award 2019). Eva's piece *Maxwell House* was performed as part of the Abbey Theatre's *Dear Ireland* project in April 2020.

Eva runs her own company Sunday's Child, with Hildegard Ryan. Eva has won various awards for her work including Best Emerging Artist Award 2012 (Edinburgh Fringe), First Fortnight Award 2014 (Dublin Fringe), Argus Angel Award 2015 (Brighton Fringe), Fishamble Award for Best New Writing 2015, Best Theatre Award 2017 (Adelaide Fringe), Scotsman Fringe First Award in 2019 (Edinburgh Fringe) and the Summerhall Lustrum Award 2019 (Edinburgh Fringe).

Her play *Overshadowed* was adapted for television by BBC Three and Rollem productions, directed by Hildegard Ryan. It won Best Drama at the Mind Media Awards 2019.

Eva has also written for radio. Her play *My Name is Saoirse* was adapted for radio by RTÉ Radio 1 and Eva's short story *The Midnight Sandwich* was aired on BBC Radio 4.